GOD'S LOVE

By Ng

Published by
Filament Publishing Ltd
16 Croydon Road, Waddon, Croydon,
Surrey, CR0 4PA, United Kingdom.
www.filamentpublishing.com
Telephone: +44 (0)20 8688 2598

© 2018 Ng

ISBN 978-1-912635-49-8
Printed by IngramSpark

Ng has asserted the right under the Copyright,
Designs and Patents Act 1988 to be identified as the
author of this work.

All rights reserved.
No part of this book may be reproduced in any
way without the prior written permission from the
publishers.

CONTENTS

About the Author	4
Preface	5
Introduction	6
Chapter One: The Meaning of Love	7
Chapter Two: Understanding Types of Love	15
Chapter Three: Bible Verses of Love	38
Conclusion	55

ABOUT THE AUTHOR

Ng is an Author, Artist and Singer-Songwriter.

PREFACE

Dictionary meaning of Love: a strong feeling of affection.
"Babies fill parents with intense feelings of love"
Synonyms: deep affection, fondness, tenderness, warmth, intimacy, attachment, endearment

My understanding of love is seeking to sacrifice for someone or your spouse and keeping to the dos and don'ts of relationship.

Love means loving someone without any IFs and BUTs, where you invest in all your efforts, care and concern for the person you love. Love is selfless and doesn't seek any personal gains in return. Also, there are no strict rules or exact meanings of love. The purpose of love varies from person to person, depending on their feelings and experiences.

INTRODUCTION

Love means giving complete care to someone without expecting anything in return. It's the most sacred feeling, as per my belief. This feeling provides an immense happiness and satisfaction within that you cannot precisely describe in words. Love is what you feel from within; it can be in any relationship let it be motherly love or the love of friendship. One gives someone a feeling to count on him by going the extra mile for her/him, by ensuring that she/he doesn't feel alone. By doing so, one eventually feels happy and at peace from the heart. Loving someone can hurt sometimes, but it's the only thing that keeps you alive with all its sweet feelings.

CHAPTER ONE
The Meaning of Love

Everyone in the world is affected by relationships, and love forms an important part of any relationship. The more you improve in relating with your spouse and others around you, the better your life. This means that your relationships affect your entire life.

Love is misunderstood by many, especially in marriage, dating, courtship, divorce and amongst families. Love has authority in relationships. There are many important decisions one can make in life and *'marriage'* is one of them.

You can decide to buy a good car and a house or have everything money can buy, but have a horrible marriage. When you spend so much money on a house and spend less time loving and building up your marriage, then the car or house will not be a conducive a place for you or Spouse. Hence, who to love and marriage becomes the most important decision one can make in life.

Unfortunately, some people's car last longer than their relationships because they spend more time chasing ideas on how to get their licence and to start driving. The reason you go for a driving lesson and test is because it is required by the law of the land before you can drive.

On the other hand, most people go into a marriage without adequate preparations on how to love and sustain a lasting relationship. It becomes easy for you to drive a car and you find it difficult to live with your spouse.

The majority of people are products of a broken heart due to a bad marriage. And you are wondering what is going on with your love life and spouse.

Your marriage can either make or mar your life and that's the reason you prayerfully and watchfully choose a partner so that you do not have any cause to regret it.

Marriage is not something one should rush into because it is a lifetime commitment. There is nowhere in the Bible that states that you must be married. You can choose to be married or choose not: it is not a requirement by God. However, I believe in a good relationship which can lead to marriage because it sometimes helps to keep you in check and committed.

Many relationship counsellors, such as Myles Munroe, are of the opinion that God doesn't choose your life partner for you because you will blame him if anything goes wrong.

Nevertheless, I think that God can guide you if you pray just like every other heart desire. When you ask God for something, he guides you into achieving it. The problem is that sometimes, sin and disobedience to his instructions might hinder one from achieving understanding God's instruction. The sin and disobedience apply to any heart desire, such as car, food, money, and much more.

The major things that God gives to guide or help us in decision making with respect to your life partner is

- Holy spirit
- God's word

We get married to people because we feel we are in love with the person. This makes love the foundation of a relationship.

Love does not make marriage work, it's part of the attributes one should have in a marriage or relationship. Do not get married solely because you love someone or the person told you sweet words. Do not be deceived when people tell you that love is all that matters for a relationship to work out.

For example, you can love an aircraft and you are not able to fly it. The fact that you do not know how to use it makes you unfit to fly the aircraft. In marriage, there is a difference between loving someone but you don't know how to manage or live with this person.

Love does not keep marriage together and most people who are divorced can acknowledge to the fact love alone does not sustain a marriage. A divorced couple was once in love with one another. They did not wake up one day to marry without having mutual feelings for one another in the past. However, other problems in the relationship were greater than the love they had for each other. For example, these problems could be:

- Infidelity
- Mental abuse
- Emotional abuse
- Financial insolvent
- Irresponsibility
- Spiritual problems

The fact remains that something came into the relationship that is stronger than the love they once professed to one another. Hence, love on its own cannot make a marriage successful.

Dr Myles Munroe is of the opinion that ***'a successful marriage is an application of knowledge and not the exchange of love'.***

The above statement is true because you need wisdom from God to resolve certain matters that may arise in the time you are married to someone.

You can be in love all you want or express your feelings with someone but it doesn't make the person right for you in marriage.

There is more to a marriage than what and how you feel for this person.

> Proverbs 4:7, *'Wisdom is the principal thing; therefore, get wisdom: and with all thy getting get understanding'*

The above scripture simply explains that you should not get LOVE but gain more knowledge to enjoy your spouse. This knowledge involves the ability to understand his or her requirements and what he or she loves.

You want to understand what a man requires from woman and what a woman requires from a man. You should be able to know how to manage emotions such as anger, happiness, loneliness, bereavement, and other emotional states that one might come across in relating with their spouse.

You need to be able to understand how to manage:

- Unfaithfulness
- Broken trust
- Lack of commitment
- Lack of love
- Lack of mutual respect

You need to do this in order to have a successful relationship.

Love cannot help you to manage the aforementioned attributes, rather it is part of what makes up a relationship.

No marriage is irretrievable. What happens is that people get tired of trying to fix their problems or they do not have the knowledge to fix their problems. No wonder the Bible explains in Hosea 4:6,

> ***'My people are destroyed because of lack of knowledge'***

The word ***'knowledge'*** applies to all areas of life including marriage and relationship.

God went further to explain in Hosea 4:7,

> ***'that because you rejected knowledge that he will reject you'***

To be ignorant becomes a choice because you should make out time to gain the necessary knowledge to manage your relationship or spouse. There are books and videos where you can gain knowledge on how to manage your affairs. However, people don't want to spend time reading or watching videos that can be of help to them.

How can you know how to manage anything or a car without going through a driving school or training? The solution to the problem you are facing in your relationship could be found in a book you have not read lying on your bookshelf, or a video, or even the Bible. Thus, knowledge is acquired through what you hear and see, as well as people you associate yourself with. However, we humans reject knowledge, and God explains that he will reject us as well.

For example, when you go for a marriage talk or relationship show and you gain information relevant to your spouse or the person you are dating, suddenly, you say to yourself, "He should have been here to hear this." Now what happened at that point is your spouse or the person you are dating has missed an opportunity to gain information that can help your relationship in one way or the other.

God went further to explain the fact that Ignorance or lack of knowledge is generational. He explains in Hosea that if you reject knowledge, I will you and your children. Thus, what you do not know about marriage and relationship or any given area is transferred to your kids.

If you are not able to stay married and solve it, your children will not be able to manage theirs because they learn from you.

You should be able to learn or read for your unborn children. The more you learn, the better they learn, but the less you learn, the less they will eventually know about life and relationships.

The most misused element of relationship is **LOVE**. We do not understand the concept of love. We are struggling to trust people because we are unrealistic of the true meaning of love. The more you put value on something, the more you feel the need. Preserve it well.

God loves you because he looks at you and sees himself, hence the reason the Bible recorded that we were made in God's image and likeness (Genesis 1:27)

CHAPTER 2
Understanding Types of Love

There are diverse kinds of love.

1. Eros love, or sexual kind of love
2. Philia, or friendship, love occurring between two friends
3. Storge, or familial, love is a love between parents and siblings
4. Agape love. Agape kind of love is not a normal kind of love. It is a love that forgives infidelity. You can not forgive unfaithfulness with eros love, friendship love or philia love. Agape love forgives a person of any offence because that is the kind of love Jesus has for you and I.

If your spouse commits adultery on you, you cannot imagine sleeping with them and you are scared of contracting any sexually transmitted diseases, then your mind starts playing tricks on you. **Eros love** is now out of the way here and it is unable to help you forgive your spouse.

The only way to love your spouse, regardless of what he or she may have done to you, is the **agape** kind of love. You have to do what Jesus did and what he is still doing to date. The Bible records in Romans 5:8 that;

'while we were yet sinners, Christ died for us'.

That's a **tough love**. It is a love that ignores all rebellion and problems. The agape love has to be in the believer, not in the word, but you might not be able to do it because it is tough for you.

Agape love is what makes a relationship sustainable. You can not experience God's idea of marriage which is **'till death do us part'** without using God's material (agape love). Everything else will fail but agape kind of love will not fail you.

Love is not emotions. Emotions, according to Myles Munroe, is a chemical. He is of the opinion that when you feel for someone, that is a chemical reaction. The major disadvantage of chemicals in body is that they change frequently, every five seconds in the body.

That's the reason that when you see a handsome guy or a beautiful lady, you feel so excited because the chemicals in your body react to the looks of the individual which goes straight to your brain. The result of that emotion will be a smile to the person from you. The excitement you feel at that time is adrenaline, and not love.

If you fall in love based on adrenaline, which most people call **infatuation**, then we can get the first person, second person, third person and fourth person. Now, what are you going to do with the first one? That's the reason people commit adultery.

Some people who have been engaged to marry another person break off their engagement because they are confusing adrenaline with love. They are confused by the emotions in their body and chemical reactions. Therefore, love is not emotion.

Furthermore, love is a choice. You have to choose to love because love is the understanding value of another thing. When you love something, you put a value on it.

For example, if you buy a dress for £200, you will want to handle such dress with care because of the value or worth of the dress.

Value is measured by what you are going to pay for something. When you pay for something, that's the value you gave it.

What did God pay to have you? He paid his own image on the cross and died on the cross for your sake. That's how much he loves you.

If someone claims they love you, then their value is measured by what they are willing to give up for you. God loves you so much that He gave up his son for you; can you meet someone who is willing to do that for you?

A woman will give up all the men around her past when she decides to marry you. Well that's value; it's a choice. The men that wanted her didn't go away. They still live on the planet; however, she always remembered that she made a choice.

This woman you claim you love, what did you cancel for her?

If your wife has to compete with your mother, then she is not the most valuable person in your life. Sometimes, your wife wants to have a conversation with you, and your mother calls. You have a choice either to pick her call or speak to your wife first. My response will be to you at that point is to ask your mother to seek permission from your wife to see you (the son). At that point, all you are doing is to protect your wife which shows how valuable she is to you. People respect your wife according to the value you place on her.

The Bible never said you should stay with your mother and father. The Bible says that you should leave your parents and cleave to your wife.

Genesis 2:24 says,

> ***Therefore shall a man leave his father and his mother, and shall cleave unto his wife: and they shall be one flesh.***

This means that if you treat your wife badly, you are doing yourself because the above scripture explains that the two shall become one flesh. If you choose to disrespect your wife before your parents or family, then you are indirectly disrespecting yourself because you are one flesh.

Most times, the choice you make as to who to marry is yours as a man. Your family may not like your chosen bride but do not forget that the choice is yours. They cannot choose for you who to marry or whom not to.

We think two people (male and female) bring two families together but it's not right because it invites interference into the home.

Some people are divorced today because of in-laws that became outlaws. No family member should just drop in on you if you are married. Your relatives are third parties to your home. Do not make them a priority or more important than your spouse.

Do not confuse your feelings with love. Take away every form of feelings from your marriage and relationship because feelings do not work.

In John 13:34, the Bible records that,

> *'a new commandment I give unto you that you love one another as I have loved you'*

Also, John 15:12 says,

> ***'Love each other as I have loved you'***

You will realise in the above scriptures, that it is a law. God keeps repeating the fact that he wants us to love one another as he has loved us.

In addition to the above scriptures, John 14:15, the Bible says that

> ***'if you love me, keep my commandments. If love God, you do good to those people that despise, abuse and hate you.'***

Do not consider sex as love; they are never the same. If someone tells you they love you and have sex with you, the person doesn't love you. The person will just use you to satisfy their sexual want.

In the society, people call sex ***'making love'*** which means it doesn't exist. What do you mean 'make love'? This means that you do not have 'it'. Hence, they make it (the love) for 45 minutes and don't want to talk to you anymore for weeks. It's not love.

Galatians 5:14 explains that the entire law is fulfilled by a single command; love your neighbour as thyself.

Furthermore, Galatians 5:22 says that the fruit of the spirit is love which means that love is not a *GIFT*, it's a fruit of the spirit. In the entire Bible, there is nothing such as *gift of love*. Love is found in you by God's grace.

When you give your life to Jesus, you automatically have the holy spirit because the Bible affirms 'that he will send us a comforter' John 14:16 (Holy spirit).

Having the holy spirit does not instantly make you have love in your heart, or rather you can have the love in your heart and not know how to use it or activate it. You can have a complete car tool set and your car breaks down and you do not know how to use it, then your car will be parked at your house with your tool set looking at you in a corner of your home.

Having the love of God is not the same as having the knowledge to fix stuff or something.

That's the reason you need this teaching to help you understand what to do. Everyone still loved the person they divorced even up until the date but the issue was you didn't have the necessary knowledge to handle your relationship or marriage, so you got tired and divorced.

Knowledge is required to sustain a relationship. People divorce not because they do not love each other, but because they do not have the knowledge which brought about so much misunderstandings amongst the couple. Sometimes, you hear people say 'I love you but I don't know when I hurt or didn't mean to hurt you'. All they are trying to say at that point is that they have agape love in their heart for you but do not have the adequate knowledge to manage you. That's why you need knowledge. Do not get married based on love.

1 John 4:7-8 says that,

> ***'Dear friends let us love one another because love comes from God [agape]. Anyone who loves has been born from God. God is love and whoever lives in love lives in God'.***

This means that you need to have an intimacy with God in order to have genuine love towards yourself and your spouse.

Love is a decision to commit to meet another person's needs for the rest of their lives without expectation, and that is a high order.

If someone falls in love with you based on **philia love**, which is friendship love, it means 'You treat me nice and I treat you nice. The moment you stop treating me nice, I will not be nice to you anymore'.

Eros love says, 'You give me money and I give you sex. No money, no sex'. You have expectations there so that's not love. **Philia love** says that we will remain friends as long as you do not hurt me and so there is an expectation. However, **Agape love** is a strange kind of love because it has no expectation, whereas all the other kinds of love have expectations. Therefore, love is *'caring for a person'*. The word **Caring**, according to Dr Myles Munroe, is defined as anticipating a need and meeting it right now.

When you care about someone, you study what they need tomorrow and give it to them today. You anticipate that your child or spouse needs a pair of shoes for next week and you buy it this week. For example, God says in Jeremiah 29:11 that the thoughts he thinks towards us is of good and not of evil to give us an expected end. The previous statement means that God goes ahead to make every rough way straight. The word caring means that I don't let you ask for anything. If someone cares for you, they find out what you are needing next in life and provide it for you. The person makes plans ahead for you.

The Bible says to *'cast all our cares upon the lord for he cares for us'* (1 Peter 5:7). This means that God cares for your need even before you ask. He says that while you are asking, he will do it for you. God died for you when you were a sinner (Romans 5:8).

He didn't die for you after you had repented. In other words, God cared for you long before you repented from your evil ways. He shows you love even before you asked or ever knew him and still loves sinners waiting patiently for them to give their life to Jesus.

God's standard of marriage explains that when you become engaged to someone, you have made a lifetime commitment to take care of the person and his or her needs without expecting anything in return. Men do pay dowry after an engagement to stay married to their wives.

A 'dowry' means *care*. You go back and prepare a place for the person you want to marry, such as house, car, washing machine and other household equipment, in preparation for your forthcoming bride. That is care.

For example, who wakes up and decides to marry, claiming he will love and care for a woman, when he does not have a job or have the ability to take care of himself because he still lives with his mother and is eating her food? That man is not ready to care because you need to be able to take care of yourself (basic needs) before you can care for another.

There is no need engaging a woman when you do not have a job or financial ability to take care of yourself and basic need, as having a relationship or going into a marriage is a lifetime commitment. You will find it difficult to fulfil the requirement of love if you do not have a source of income because love, simply put, means *'a lifetime commitment to meet another's need and expect nothing in return'*. Therefore, if a guy walks up to a lady and says *'I love you'*, you are just saying I am willing to help you without anything in return.

Jesus Christ did not just save you and I. He supplies all our needs according to his riches in glory by Christ Jesus.

Some people might have to remain single for life because their demands are way too high for anyone to meet, whereas some women are married to men that are stingy because they have to beg for a pair of shoes for three weeks. Love is a high order; you need to find out if the person you want to marry has the capacity to meet your demands. If your demand is too high for the men that are coming for you, then you might as well remain single, rather than getting frustrated into the marriage later and opting out. Therefore, it's either you are willing to lower your needs or standards, or hold on until the person that has the ability to care for you comes, which can take ages or come quickly.

Some men marry women that are parasites. They lose everything they have to these women. These set of women do not bring anything good to the marriage.

Love is the manifestation of the inherent love of God. True love is found in a human when God's kind of agape flows through humans.

Agape love means true love that does not have any reason. If you can find a reason why you love someone, you cancel the love.

If you read the whole of the Bible, you can not find one reason why God loves us because the minute you give a reason, then it is no longer love. If someone tells you they love you, ask the person why.

If the person gives you a reason, then it's not true love because **'true love does not have a reason'**. Their response to the question might destroy the relationship. Thus, the reason we should realise that genuine love is rare amongst human. The nature of human beings is deceptive and we want something in return for a good will. However, God's kind of love is real and pure without expectations or desire.

I want you to try and ask the person you are engaged to or your spouse why he or she loves you. You will be shocked at what you will hear. It's unfortunate that most Christians marry or go into a relationship because of mutual benefit they can receive from another and not the actual love.

If the person has a reason for loving you, it's bad because when that thing goes, the love dies. For example, someone loves you because you have a good job. When the job goes, the love the person for you dies automatically. "I love you because you earn so much money but unfortunately the money is gone now, hence the love is gone." You have to retain that job or stay financially buoyant; it's a condition.

Whenever there is a reason for love, there is *'a condition'*. Wherever there is a condition, there are **expectations** and if that expectation is not forthcoming, the relationship **gets worse**. The expectation brings in frustration if it is not being given by other party.

Some men married a woman because she has curves and a beautiful shape. However, after she has three children and the curves disappears, he starts running after high school girls because he never loved his wife in the first place. The reason and condition he married her for was because she had curves and a shape. The expectations which are not met leads to quarrels, which will eventually lead to division (divorce). Divorce means divided vision (division). Jesus says that in Mark 3:25,

'any house divided against itself cannot stand'

Sometimes, we cannot always control life and that's why it is not good to have conditions with love. This means that once the gifts, money and all reasons why you claim you love the person is gone, your visions become different and eventually leads to countless quarrels.

Some women suffer every day to go and work because their husband refused to work. These set of women become under pressure. Divorce means death; something died in the relationship but people do not understand it. The happiness, peace or love may have died by someone or something stronger than normal.

For love and marriage to last, you have to get rid of the reason why you love your spouse. Conditions destroy not just the couple but the children's perception of marriage and relationship. If you divorce today, there is a high tendency that your children will follow the same part in life.

God is not happy when couples break the vows they made at the altar to themselves.

The phrase 'till death do us part' is a vow which most people do not fulfil. One of the ways they do not fulfil this is by leaving one another through a divorce.

The Bible explains that it is better not to vow than to vow and not fulfil it. It is easier to break a promise but it is not good to break a vow.

Vows are meant to be kept and not broken. A vow attracts judgement. You should never be found saying **'why did I marry you?'** or **'I regret marrying you'**. When you say that, you have broken your vow.

For richer for poorer, in sickness and in health, till death do us part. Unfortunately, most of us do not mean or keep to our words.

When challenges come in our marriage, we find it difficult to keep to our vows.

God gives us wisdom on how to face challenges in our relationship.

When you make a vow to God, you have given God the power to judge you. Hence, you should take your time before rushing down to the altar. The problem is that we do not fear God, because the fear of God enables you not take certain steps without a careful thought about it. When you fear God, you will consult him first before getting married to anyone while you watch and pray if there are physical signs or behaviours in the person that will enable you to go ahead with the relationship or not.

Dr Myles Munroe is of the opinion that promises are made to humans and can be broken. When someone tells you, "I love you," they need to say that to God. They need to say that to God Almighty, which becomes a vow and it should be kept. Vows have consequences and that is when you make a vow to your spouse 'to love in sickness and in health, for richer, for poorer, till death do us part,' the death in the above statement is the judgement. The moment you make a vow before God to marry someone, you have told God to judge you when you do not keep to the vow. All you have said to God by making the above statement is that "you are permitted to kill me if I do not keep to the above covenant"

The difference between vows and promises is that the former has an inherent judgement and the latter can be broken without judgement from God or any consequences.

When you are engaged to be married to someone, you have only made a promise, but when you have done a wedding at the altar of God and made promises at the same time, then you have chosen a part of no return. You can pull out of an engagement without consequences but you cannot pull out of a marriage without judgement. Why? Because you made a vow to your spouse before God.

Paul in the Bible is of the opinion that when you are married, stay married and fight for it. Do all your best to put your marriage back together. You do not want God to judge you, but if you have already divorced and you want to go the second time, read this book ten times before you make a choice to avoid more problems for yourself.

Reasons you should not add conditions to love

A love and marriage based on conditions will eventually lead to a broken home. When a marriage breaks, it has a poor effect on the couple, children and the society at large. Love is so deep; we are still in Eros kind of love and we need to upgrade to the kingdom principles of love. If you want to destroy a society, then give conditions to your love. Your relationship is personal but it is not private. God's kingdom has its citizenship and laws that guide love and these are as follows.

A male is the head of a marriage, yes, but he has to behave exactly the way he expects the wife to be. For example, Jesus is the head of any relationship if you let him in. He asks you to do things or exhibit the attributes he has, and not the other way around. He should practise what he preaches.

If you keep to the above rules, you cannot miss 'love' in your life, doing things exactly the way your spouse desires as long as it's in line with God's will for your life and it's not at the detriment of your health.

How to genuinely love

We as humans mistake the idea of love for attachment. When you get used to the company of someone, you assume that you love the person. The clinging and grasping we exhibit towards one another is not love. For me, you are simply attached to the person.

For example, when a baby gets used to hugs, cuddles and clings to her mother or caregiver, the baby does not know what love means at that point. However, the baby becomes so attached to this individual because they spent more time together and maybe gets cuddles from the person.

Attachment and love are slightly related because love comes with care, peace and sometimes cuddles between couples or families. However, there is a big difference between the two.

Being attached to someone causes pain sometimes because the more you grasp to this individual, the more you fear to lose the person. If you eventually lose this person, then you will suffer.

Genuine love seeks to make another happy from within, whereas attachment expects you to make the other person happy.

This might sound difficult, but you need to love another no matter what they do to you. You might not be able to exhibit that love if you do not have the fruits of the holy spirit (Galatians 5:22-23). I am not preaching church or religion here, all I am propagating at this point is genuine relationship with the holy spirit and getting his fruits which includes love, long-suffering, kindness, peace, joy, gentleness, faithfulness, self- control.

Having the above attributes will help you relate well with your spouse as well as colleagues, church members, friends and even your enemies.

I believe that the first person we should be attached to is God.

If you are a God addict, you will realise your ability to love and relate with your spouse and everyone around you.

Some people go into a relationship to get fulfilled, whereas a relationship should be made up of two already fulfilled individuals coming together to appreciate themselves.

The above fulfilment comes from building a personal relationship with Jesus who makes you understand and feel fulfilled about yourself.

Most relationships become boring after a while, if not nurtured.

Love is when you are committed to love daily, physically and emotionally; it is not a mere feeling as some people believe. It's hard work, a conscious effort and a choice.

Individuals get tired and quit relationships when they face challenges. I remember some time ago, I wanted to leave my husband because of challenges we faced. I was fed up with everything but the spirit reminded me that I will definitely face challenges if I move on into another relationship in the future. And that is true.

Relationships have their ups and downs. Your love for your spouse might feel as though it is gone but that's not the case. You both might be going through a process and the smiles, laughs and fun times shall return.

People quit relationships when a great positive change is about to happen for them in their lives and relationship. A little patience might solve your age-long problems.

Most researchers get their ideas from the Bible. However, most of them refuse to acknowledge the fact that God himself is love and it's difficult to define love without God and his ideas.

Some people do not want to sound religious but the fact remains that the essence of Christianity, Bible and God is love.

It's all about love. Where there is love, you find the fruits of the holy spirit which is peace, joy, gentleness (Galatians 5:22-23)

The easiest way to exhibit and sustain love is by praying constantly to have the fruits of the holy spirit in our lives. When you have these fruits, it will enable you to love and treat yourself and your spouse well, your children, and colleagues as well.

"Why should I love myself?" The Importance of loving yourself

The most important pursuit in life is to be single in life and totally single, says Dr Myles Munroe. Singleness is the foundation of all relationships, including you and your boss, citizens and politicians, you and your children, friends, colleagues, and most importantly, an intimate relationship between man and wife. Just any kind of relationship. All the aforementioned relationships start from your single state.

Singleness determines your relationship in the social (friends, church members), personal (marriage, dating, children, family) and professional (boss, colleagues) environments. If you find yourself struggling in relating with your colleagues at work, then you are having a **SINGLENESS PROBLEM**. You might find it hard to believe but it's the truth. Also, if you and your spouse are having problems all the time, then you are having a singleness problem.

What does this mean?

I will start by using a concept that states that the most important relationship is **INTRAPERSONAL RELATIONSHIP** and not **INTERPERSONAL RELATIONSHIP**.

Most of our aims as individuals is to get along with other people (interpersonal relationship) but that is the wrong ideology. Our major focus is to develop a relationship with ourselves (intrapersonal relationship), which means understanding your person. Understanding oneself is important. Understand your needs and what works and then you will pick up interest in learning, or understanding your colleagues, family, friends, spouses, children and any other kind of relationship.

The average person on this planet does not know themselves. All they do is put on the image of others, trying to be and please others. Instead of you developing a concept for yourself, you create *'others concept'* about you (in dressing, speaking, looks, walk, smile).

Self-knowledge becomes the key to all relationships. Understanding yourself is a key for you to enjoy a blissful relationship. It is pertinent for you to identify your strengths and weakness.

Strengths are positive aspect of your life whilst your weaknesses pushes towards the negative. If you do not realise your negative attributes, it will eventually become a big hindrance to your relationship with spouse, family, children, boss and the person you are dating. Also, it will be difficult for you to change because you don't know your weakness. Thus, you cannot change what you don't know.

Sometimes, we do something and we deny it and never desire to tell ourselves the truth. Rather, we start looking for who to blame for our actions and fail to take responsibility for what we have done. You consciously make an effort not to blame anyone for your mistakes in life.

The most important person to love is not other people, but yourself. This is not selfishness but rather it is getting to a place where you appreciate and have value for yourself which you will transfer to others.

The Bible posits that you should love your neighbour as thyself (Matthew 22:36-40), hence you need to love yourself first because you cannot give what you don't have.

Loving yourself is the most important aspect of stress.

If you are stressed, you can not take care of your children and husband which has a negative impact on your relationship.

If you love yourself, you will take care of your weight, meals and shape, and in return you can take care of your children. It is difficult to advise your children against gluttony, smoking or drinking when you do the same. For example, I scolded my little girl when she does wrong. I caught her scolding her brother in the same manner.

CHAPTER 3
Bible Verses of Love

Love is patient and kind; love does not envy or boast; it is not arrogant or rude. It does not insist on its own way; it is not irritable or resentful; it does not rejoice at wrongdoing, but rejoices with the truth. Love bears all things, believes all things, hopes all things, endures all things. Love never ends. As for prophecies, they will pass away; as for tongues, they will cease; as for knowledge, it will pass away.

1 Corinthians 16:14 ESV, ***Let all that you do be done in love.***

1 John 4:8 ESV, ***Anyone who does not love does not know God, because God is love.***

John 13:34-35 ESV, ***A new commandment I give to you, that you love one another: just as I have loved you, you also are to love one another. By this all people will know that you are my disciples, if you have love for one another."***

John 3:16 ESV, ***"For God so loved the world, that he gave his only Son, that whoever believes in him should not perish but have eternal life.***

Colossians 3:14 ESV, *And above all these put on love, which binds everything together in perfect harmony.*

1 Peter 4:8 ESV, *Above all, keep loving one another earnestly, since love covers a multitude of sins.*

John 15:13 ESV, *Greater love has no one than this, that someone lay down his life for his friends.*

Mark 12:29-31, *Jesus answered, "The most important is, 'Hear, O Israel: The Lord our God, the Lord is one. And you shall love the Lord your God with all your heart and with all your soul and with all your mind and with all your strength.' The second is this: 'You shall love your neighbour as yourself.' There is no other commandment greater than these."*

Matthew 22:36-40, *"Teacher, which is the great commandment in the Law?" And he said to him, "You shall love the Lord your God with all your heart and with all your soul and with all your mind. This is the great and first commandment. And a second is like it: You shall love your neighbour as yourself. On these two commandments depend all the Law and the Prophets."*

1 Corinthians 13:13 ESV, *So now faith, hope, and love abide, these three; but the greatest of these is love.*

1 John 4:19 ESV, *We love because he first loved us.*

1 John 4:18 ESV, *There is no fear in love, but perfect love casts out fear. For fear has to do with punishment, and whoever fears has not been perfected in love.*

1 John 4:7 ESV, *Beloved, let us love one another, for love is from God, and whoever loves has been born of God and knows God.*

1 Corinthians 13:1-5 ESV, *If I speak in the tongues of men and of angels, but have not love, I am a noisy gong or a clanging cymbal. And if I have prophetic powers, and understand all mysteries and all knowledge, and if I have all faith, so as to remove mountains, but have not love, I am nothing. If I give away all I have, and if I deliver up my body to be burned, but have not love, I gain nothing. Love is patient and kind; love does not envy or boast; it is not arrogant or rude. It does not insist on its own way; it is not irritable or resentful;*

Proverbs 10:12 ESV, *Hatred stirs up strife, but love covers all offenses.*

Ephesians 5:25 ESV, *Husbands, love your wives, as Christ loved the church and gave himself up for her,*

John 14:15 ESV, *"If you love me, you will keep my commandments.*

Ephesians 4:2 ESV, *With all humility and gentleness, with patience, bearing with one another in love,*

Romans 5:8 ESV, *But God shows his love for us in that while we were still sinners, Christ died for us.*

Romans 12:9 ESV, *Let love be genuine. Abhor what is evil; hold fast to what is good.*

Proverbs 17:17 ESV, *A friend loves at all times, and a brother is born for adversity.*

Luke 6:35 ESV, *But love your enemies, and do good, and lend, expecting nothing in return, and your reward will be great, and you will be sons of the Most High, for he is kind to the ungrateful and the evil.*

1 John 4:16 ESV, *So we have come to know and to believe the love that God has for us. God is love, and whoever abides in love abides in God, and God abides in him.*

1 Corinthians 13:4-7 ESV, *Love is patient and kind; love does not envy or boast; it is not arrogant or rude. It does not insist on its own way; it is not irritable or resentful; it does not rejoice at wrong doing, but rejoices with the truth. Love bears all things, believes all things, hopes all things, endures all things.*

Romans 12:10 ESV, *Love one another with brotherly affection. Outdo one another in showing honour.*

Romans 13:8 ESV, *Owe no one anything, except to love each other, for the one who loves another has fulfilled the law.*

1 John 3:1 ESV, *See what kind of love the Father has given to us, that we should be called children of God; and so we are. The reason why the world does not know us is that it did not know him.*

1 John 3:18 ESV, *Little children, let us not love in word or talk but in deed and in truth.*

Ephesians 5:33 ESV, *However, let each one of you love his wife as himself, and let the wife see that she respects her husband.*

Proverbs 17:9 ESV, *Whoever covers an offense seeks love, but he who repeats a matter separates close friends.*

Mark 12:31 ESV, *The second is this: 'You shall love your neighbour as yourself.' There is no other commandment greater than these."*

Galatians 5:22 ESV, *But the fruit of the Spirit is love, joy, peace, patience, kindness, goodness, faithfulness*

Matthew 22:37-39 ESV, *And he said to him, "You shall love the Lord your God with all your heart and with all your soul and with all your mind. This is the great and first commandment. And a second is like it: You shall love your neighbour as yourself.*

Romans 13:10 ESV, *Love does no wrong to a neighbour; therefore love is the fulfilling of the law.*

Galatians 2:20 ESV, *I have been crucified with Christ. It is no longer I who live, but Christ who lives in me. And the life I now live in the flesh I live by faith in the Son of God, who loved me and gave himself for me.*

Luke 6:31 ESV, *And as you wish that others would do to you, do so to them.*

Romans 8:37-39 ESV, *No, in all these things we are more than conquerors through him who loved us. For I am sure that neither death nor life, nor angels nor rulers, nor things present nor things to come, nor powers, nor height nor depth, nor anything else in all creation, will be able to separate us from the love of God in Christ Jesus our Lord.*

John 14:21 ESV, *Whoever has my commandments and keeps them, he it is who loves me. And he who loves me will be loved by my Father, and I will love him and manifest myself to him."*

Matthew 6:24 ESV, *"No one can serve two masters, for either he will hate the one and love the other, or he will be devoted to the one and despise the other. You cannot serve God and money.*

1 Corinthians 13:2 ESV, *And if I have prophetic powers, and understand all mysteries and all knowledge, and if I have all faith, so as to remove mountains, but have not love, I am nothing.*

John 15:12 ESV, *"This is my commandment, that you love one another as I have loved you.*

Matthew 22:37 ESV, *And he said to him, "You shall love the Lord your God with all your heart and with all your soul and with all your mind.*

Deuteronomy 7:9 ESV, *Know therefore that the Lord your God is God, the faithful God who keeps covenant and steadfast love with those who love him and keep his commandments, to a thousand generations*

John 14:23 ESV, *Jesus answered him, "If anyone loves me, he will keep my word, and my Father will love him, and we will come to him and make our home with him.*

Matthew 5:44-48 ESV, *But I say to you, Love your enemies and pray for those who persecute you, so that you may be sons of your Father who is in heaven. For he makes his sun rise on the evil and on the good, and sends rain on the just and on the unjust. For if you love those who love you, what reward do you have? Do not even the tax collectors do the same? And if you greet only your brothers, what more are you doing than others? Do not even the Gentiles do the same? You therefore must be perfect, as your heavenly Father is perfect.*

Genesis 29:20 ESV, *So Jacob served seven years for Rachel, and they seemed to him but a few days because of the love he had for her.*

Romans 8:28 ESV, *And we know that for those who love God all things work together for good, for those who are called according to his purpose.*

1 John 4:20 ESV, *If anyone says, "I love God," and hates his brother, he is a liar; for he who does not love his brother whom he has seen cannot love God whom he has not seen.*

Zephaniah 3:17 ESV, *The Lord your God is in your midst, a mighty one who will save; he will rejoice over you with gladness; he will quiet you by his love; he will exult over you with loud singing.*

1 Peter 5:6-7 ESV, *Humble yourselves, therefore, under the mighty hand of God so that at the proper time he may exalt you, casting all your anxieties on him, because he cares for you.*

James 2:8 ESV, *If you really fulfil the royal law according to the Scripture, "You shall love your neighbour as yourself," you are doing well.*

Song of Solomon 8:6-7 ESV, ***Set me as a seal upon your heart, as a seal upon your arm, for love is strong as death, jealousy is fierce as the grave. Its flashes are flashes of fire, the very flame of the Lord. Many waters cannot quench love, neither can floods drown it. If a man offered for love all the wealth of his house, he would be utterly despised.***

Matthew 5:22 ESV, ***But I say to you that everyone who is angry with his brother will be liable to judgment; whoever insults his brother will be liable to the council; and whoever says, 'You fool!' will be liable to the hell of fire.***

Proverbs 30:18-19 ESV, ***Three things are too wonderful for me; four I do not understand: the way of an eagle in the sky, the way of a serpent on a rock, the way of a ship on the high seas, and the way of a man with a virgin.***

Ephesians 2:4-5 ESV, ***But God, being rich in mercy, because of the great love with which he loved us, even when we were dead in our trespasses, made us alive together with Christ— by grace you have been saved***

Matthew 5:43-44 ESV, *"You have heard that it was said, 'You shall love your neighbour and hate your enemy.' But I say to you, Love your enemies and pray for those who persecute you*

Proverbs 15:17 ESV, *Better is a dinner of herbs where love is than a fattened ox and hatred with it.*

Proverbs 5:19 ESV, *A lovely deer, a graceful doe. Let her breasts fill you at all times with delight; be intoxicated always in her love.*

Leviticus 19:18 ESV, *You shall not take vengeance or bear a grudge against the sons of your own people, but you shall love your neighbour as yourself: I am the Lord.*

Philippians 2:2 ESV, *Complete my joy by being of the same mind, having the same love, being in full accord and of one mind.*

1 Corinthians 13:1-3 ESV, *If I speak in the tongues of men and of angels, but have not love, I am a noisy gong or a clanging cymbal. And if I have prophetic powers, and understand all mysteries and all knowledge, and if I have all faith, so as to remove mountains, but have not love, I am nothing. If I give away all I have, and if I deliver up my body to be burned, but have not love, I gain nothing.*

Galatians 5:22-23 ESV, *But the fruit of the Spirit is love, joy, peace, patience, kindness, goodness, faithfulness, gentleness, self-control; against such things there is no law.*

1 John 4:21 ESV, *And this commandment we have from him: whoever loves God must also love his brother.*

Galatians 5:13 ESV, *For you were called to freedom, brothers. Only do not use your freedom as an opportunity for the flesh, but through love serve one another.*

Matthew 10:37 ESV, *Whoever loves father or mother more than me is not worthy of me, and whoever loves son or daughter more than me is not worthy of me.*

1 John 4:16-19 ESV, *So we have come to know and to believe the love that God has for us. God is love, and whoever abides in love abides in God, and God abides in him. By this is love perfected with us, so that we may have confidence for the day of judgment, because as he is so also are we in this world. There is no fear in love, but perfect love casts out fear. For fear has to do with punishment, and whoever fears has not been perfected in love. We love because he first loved us.*

Song of Solomon 1:2 ESV, *Let him kiss me with the kisses of his mouth! For your love is better than wine;*

Song of Solomon 4:10 ESV, *How beautiful is your love, my sister, my bride! How much better is your love than wine, and the fragrance of your oils than any spice!*

1 Corinthians 13:4 ESV, *Love is patient and kind; love does not envy or boast; it is not arrogant*

1 Peter 1:22 ESV, *Having purified your souls by your obedience to the truth for a sincere brotherly love, love one another earnestly from a pure heart,*

Ephesians 4:32, *Be kind to one another, tender hearted, forgiving one another, as God in Christ forgave you.*

Song of Solomon 2:16, *My beloved is mine, and I am his; he grazes among the lilies.*

Ephesians 4:2-3, *With all humility and gentleness, with patience, bearing with one another in love, eager to maintain the unity of the Spirit in the bond of peace.*

2 Corinthians 5:14, *For the love of Christ controls us, because we have concluded this: that one has died for all, therefore all have died;*

Psalm 18:1, *To the choirmaster. A Psalm of David, the servant of the Lord, who addressed the words of this song to the Lord on the day when the Lord rescued him from the hand of all his enemies, and from the hand of Saul. He said: I love you, O Lord, my strength.*

Proverbs 8:17, *I love those who love me, and those who seek me diligently find me.*

Proverbs 3:3-4, *Let not steadfast love and faithfulness forsake you; bind them around your neck; write them on the tablet of your heart. So you will find favour and good success in the sight of God and man.*

Galatians 5:13-14, *For you were called to freedom, brothers. Only do not use your freedom as an opportunity for the flesh, but through love serve one another. For the whole law is fulfilled in one word: "You shall love your neighbour as yourself."*

1 John 4:11, *Beloved, if God so loved us, we also ought to love one another.*

Romans 8:35, *Who shall separate us from the love of Christ? Shall tribulation, or distress, or persecution, or famine, or nakedness, or danger, or sword?*

1 Corinthians 10:24, *Let no one seek his own good, but the good of his neighbour.*

1 John 4:12 ESV, *No one has ever seen God; if we love one another, God abides in us and his love is perfected in us.*

John 3:16-17, *"For God so loved the world, that he gave his only Son, that whoever believes in him should not perish but have eternal life. For God did not send his Son into the world to condemn the world, but in order that the world might be saved through him.*

Jeremiah 31:3, *The Lord appeared to him from far away. I have loved you with an everlasting love; therefore I have continued my faithfulness to you.*

1 Thessalonians 4:9, *Now concerning brotherly love you have no need for anyone to write to you, for you yourselves have been taught by God to love one another*

Ephesians 3:17-19, *So that Christ may dwell in your hearts through faith—that you, being rooted and grounded in love, may have strength to comprehend with all the saints what is the breadth and length and height and depth, and to know the love of Christ that surpasses knowledge, that you may be filled with all the fullness of God.*

Isaiah 43:4, *Because you are precious in my eyes, and honoured, and I love you, I give men in return for you, peoples in exchange for your life.*

Romans 5:5, *And hope does not put us to shame, because God's love has been poured into our hearts through the Holy Spirit who has been given to us.*

Psalm 63:3, *Because your steadfast love is better than life, my lips will praise you.*

1 Corinthians 13:4-5, *Love is patient and kind; love does not envy or boast; it is not arrogant or rude. It does not insist on its own way; it is not irritable or resentful;*

John 17:26, *I made known to them your name, and I will continue to make it known, that the love with which you have loved me may be in them, and I in them."*

Romans 13:8-10, *Owe no one anything, except to love each other, for the one who loves another has fulfilled the law. For the commandments, "You shall not commit adultery, You shall not murder, You shall not steal, You shall not covet," and any other commandment, are summed up in this word: "You shall love your neighbour as yourself." Love does no wrong to a neighbour; therefore love is the fulfilling of the law.*

Psalm 143:8, *Let me hear in the morning of your steadfast love, for in you I trust. Make me know the way I should go, for to you I lift up my soul.*

CONCLUSION

There are many tips that can help you have a successful marriage or relationship. These ideas are honesty, mutual respect, love, commitment, trust, and much more. Love is one but cannot sustain a relationship on its own. God's kind of love (agape) is the only type of love that can sustain a long-lasting healthy relationship.

When you have agape love for someone, it becomes easy through the help of the holy spirit to be honest, have mutual respect, commit, trust and exhibit other fruits of holy spirit towards one another.

You need to build a personal relationship with Jesus to consciously understand him and be like him. God is love and you can not genuinely love another without knowing God. Hence, when you know God, you understand love and ultimately you are able to love your spouse, family and friends, just like God.

Love God, Love yourself and Love Others
(Ng)

www.ingramcontent.com/pod-product-compliance
Lightning Source LLC
Chambersburg PA
CBHW071036080526
44587CB00015B/2649